ANIMAL PLANET

W9-BWS-796

BUGS!

JAMES BUCKLEY, JR.

BUGS!

Published by Liberty Street,
an imprint of Time Inc. Books
225 Liberty Street
New York, New York 10281

LIBERTY
STREET

LIBERTY STREET is a trademark of Time Inc.

ISBN: 978-1-68330-756-3

First edition, 2017

1 QGT 17

10 9 8 7 6 5 4 3 2 1

Some of the content in this book was originally published in *Discovery Bugopedia: The Complete Guide to Everything Bugs.*

Produced by Scout Books & Media Inc

Time Inc. Books products may be purchased for business or promotional use. For information on bulk purchases, please contact Christi Crowley in the Special Sales Department at (845) 895-9858.

To order Time Inc. Books Collector's Editions, please call (800) 327-6388, Monday through Friday, 7 a.m.–9 p.m., Central Time.

We welcome your comments and suggestions about Time Inc. Books. Please write to us at: Time Inc. Books, Attention: Book Editors, P.O. Box 62310, Tampa, Florida 33662–2310.

timeincbooks.com

Scientists have divided all the insects in the world into different orders. The insects within each order have some similar features. Insects whose names are listed in **bold** appear in Meet the Insect Orders on page 110, under the name of the order they belong to.

CONTENTS

BODY OF THE BEAST

There are nearly 1 million different species of insects in the world. They come in many shapes and sizes, but most adult insects share the same types of body parts.

Wings

Simple eye

Antenna

Compound eye

Mouth

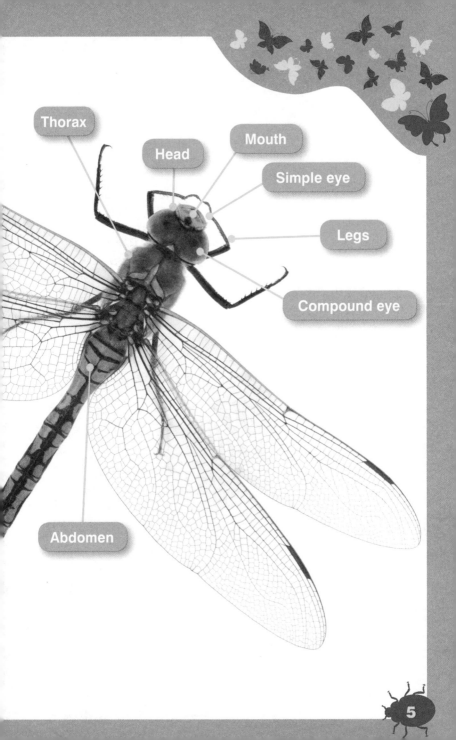

Thorax

Head

Mouth

Simple eye

Legs

Compound eye

Abdomen

BOLD AND BRIGHT There are nearly 1 million known species of insects. Each has a different body shape and color. This **elegant grasshopper's** bright colors warn predators that it is poisonous.

CHAPTER 1

WHAT MAKES AN INSECT AN INSECT?

There are nearly 1 million known species, or different kinds, of insects. There are about 10 quintillion (10,000,000,000,000,000,000) individual insects alive at any given time. There are about 7 billion human beings on Earth. That means insects outnumber us by 1 trillion to one!

Insects are all around us. They make their homes everywhere on Earth except the oceans. They can be larger than the palm of a hand. They can be so tiny that you need a microscope to see them.

Insects help plants reproduce by spreading pollen. Some insects, like grasshoppers and crickets, are considered tasty by millions of people around the world. Maggots help in crime detection and science research. Some insects are even used to treat diseases.

Insects are invertebrates, which means they do not

have bony skeletons on the inside of their bodies. Instead, they have exoskeletons. Exo means "outer." An exoskeleton is the hard shell that surrounds most of their body. The exoskeleton protects the insect's body parts.

Insects have three body parts and six legs. The three main body parts are the head, thorax, and abdomen (see pages 4-5). You can see these three parts if you look closely.

An insect's head includes its eyes. It also has a pair of antennae (an-TEN-ee). These wiggle and move to gather information about the insect's world. Like insects, antennae come in many shapes and sizes.

The insect's head also has mouthparts. As we'll see, different insects eat in different ways. What mouthparts they have depends on what they eat.

The middle body part of an insect is the thorax. All insects have six legs, which are attached to the thorax.

Each leg has several joints, and ends in a foot. Insect feet are different in different species.

Maybug

Most have some kind of sharp point to help them grab any surface.

Most insects have wings. They are attached to the thorax. Some insects, such as butterflies, have wings that are much bigger than their bodies. The wings of beetles are folded and protected by a hard cover when not being used. Others have wings that are tiny and are rarely used.

The third insect body part is the abdomen. In this part, insects digest their food. The reproductive organs needed to make more insects are in the abdomen, too.

Three body parts, six legs, and wings are what make an insect an insect.

FACT FILE: WHERE THEY LIVE

Insects live everywhere except the ocean. Here are examples of habitats where they thrive.

Blue morpho butterflies live in the rain forest of South America.

Milkweed bugs are named for the plants that grow in the North American woodlands where these insects live.

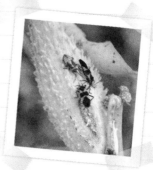

Longheaded grasshoppers are at home in grasslands in North America.

 Dung is another word for animal poop. **Dung beetles** lay their eggs inside what other animals leave behind. The African desert is one habitat where dung beetles live.

Stick insects, found everywhere except polar regions, thrive in warm climates. They camouflage (disguise  or hide) themselves among tree branches.

 **Arctic woolly bear caterpillars** can stand up to the cold. They have chemicals in their cells that keep their bodies from freezing.

HIDDEN Female **green stink bugs** lay eggs on the undersides of leaves. This protects them from weather and predators.

INSECT LIFE CYCLES

Nearly all insects begin life the same way. The adult female lays eggs. She might lay one egg at a time or a huge bunch, depending on the species. For example, a bedbug lays just one to a few eggs a day. But a termite queen can lay up to 30,000 eggs every day of her life.

Insect eggs come in many shapes and sizes. Some are oval. Others are round. The color of the egg also varies. Sometimes it helps camouflage the egg from predators by blending into its habitat.

Insects lay eggs where there will be food for their babies. Few insects stick around after laying their eggs. The female lays the eggs and then walks or flies away.

Some insects lay their eggs in water. It can take a few days or weeks for the eggs to hatch. The babies, called larvae (LAHR-vee), may live underwater after hatching. For example, mayfly larvae, called nymphs (nimfs), live underwater for two years. Then they emerge (come out) from the water as adults.

Other insects lay their eggs on plants. The undersides of leaves are a common egg-laying spot.

The eggs are sticky so they don't fall off the leaves. The leaves hide the eggs from predators. The eggs are also protected while they develop.

Many different kinds of animals hatch from eggs. Birds, for example, come out of eggs. So do many species of

Dragonflies and their relatives, the damselflies, lay eggs in or near the water.

snakes. Most of those animals look a lot like little adults when they hatch.

That's not always the case with insects. In fact, after the eggs hatch and the insect babies emerge, their next stage of growth may take days, months, or even years.

Over time, the babies go through a big change as they become adults. This change is called metamorphosis (met-ah-MORE-foh-sis). That means instead of just growing larger over time, their bodies change in a big way.

There are two types of metamorphosis: simple and complete.

Simple metamorphosis has three stages.

First, the female lays

eggs in a safe place.

Second, the eggs hatch and the
nymphs are born. The nymphs look like
mini-adults. They have the same body
shape and body parts as adults. They have
legs and antennae. They are just smaller.

Third, the insects grow. As they
grow, they shed their exoskeletons. This
is called molting. The outer shell slides

IN YOUR NEWSFEED

STICKING AROUND

INSECT FIRST AID

Caddis fly eggs hatch in
water. They then camouflage
themselves. Some spin a basket
or net out of silk and attach pebbles and other
debris to it. Researchers are looking closely
at the sticky stuff the young insects use. They
hope it will help them develop new bandages
for humans that will stick better when wet.

off and a new exoskeleton is underneath.

Some insects will molt many times as they grow. Molting stops when the insect reaches its full adult size.

Dragonflies, cockroaches, grasshoppers, and termites all go through simple metamorphosis.

Complete metamorphosis has four stages.

First, the female lays eggs in a safe place.

The empty shell this **green cicada** leaves behind as it molts looks like a hollow insect.

Second, the eggs hatch. The baby in this case is called a larva. If there are more than one, they are called larvae. Larvae are so different from their adult parents that they look like a different species. Larvae do not have wings. They have one or two body sections. Most larvae look a bit like tiny worms with legs.

Third, when the larvae have eaten enough to survive the transformation to the next stage, they stop eating. They create small bags or sacs around their bodies. Inside the sacs, the larvae are changing . . . a lot. Their bodies change shape inside the sacs.

Fourth, the insects break free from their sacs. This may take days or weeks,

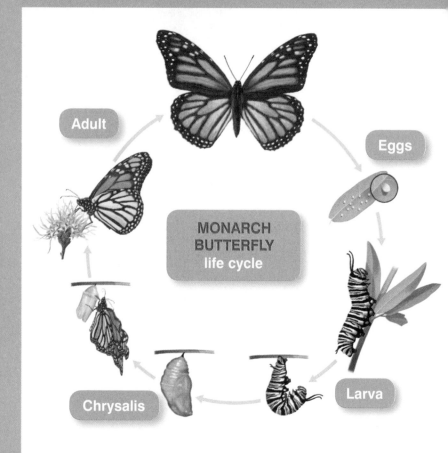

depending on the type of insect. They
are now adults. They have developed
an insect's three main body parts.
They have longer antennae.
They will often be a different
color, too.

In addition to butterflies, moths, beetles, bees and wasps, ants, and flies all go through complete metamorphosis.

LARVAL LIFE

Larvae are really good at one thing: eating. They eat a lot and grow quickly.

Larvae can't fly. Because of this, they don't wander too far from where they are born. Some larvae, such as mosquitoes, are born underwater.

The most well-known larvae come from moths and butterflies. Their larvae are called caterpillars.

Caterpillars come in many colors and varieties—but they're not always the same colors they will be as adults.

FACT FILE: A GOOEY CENTER

The change from larva to adult insect is one of nature's most amazing events.

After it's done building the chrysalis, the caterpillar, um . . . eats itself. It spits out powerful chemicals that dissolve nearly all of its body parts. The inside of a chrysalis is like caterpillar goo. It may sound gross, but what happens next is pretty cool.

Some important cells are not dissolved. These cells become parts of the butterfly. Those important cells use the goo as energy to grow and develop into different body parts of the adult insect.

Scientists have found out that the insect's airway develops first. Then the butterfly's guts grow. After a few days, wings appear.

When the butterfly has fully changed, it takes a deep breath. Air leaks into the chrysalis during the change. By inhaling this air, the butterfly's body expands. This causes the chrysalis to crack. The new butterfly wiggles out. When its wings are dry, the butterfly can fly.

Monarch butterfly metamorphosis

HANDSTAND CONTEST This **Kirby's dropwing dragonfly** looks like it's doing a handstand. That's how it cools off when it gets too warm.

DRAGONFLIES

Dragonflies have lived on Earth for more than 300 million years. Over that time, they have not changed much. Dragonflies are known as "primitive-winged" insects. Their wings function the same way they always have: They can't be folded back onto their bodies. Nearly all other insects have evolved (changed over time) to be able to fold their wings.

Dragonflies have four wings. Each wing can move on its own. Their wings

THAT'S FISHY!

Dragonfly and damselfly larvae, called naiads, are fierce. They move very quickly and have very strong jaws. They can even catch and eat small fish! When they are ready, naiads crawl out of their watery nurseries. They break out of their exoskeletons and complete their molt. Their wings unfold and their long bodies stretch out in new exoskeletons. They are ready to begin their adult lives.

After hatching, damselflies are smaller than dragonflies. Most are only an inch or so long. Unlike dragonflies, damselflies can fold their wings back along their bodies a bit. They can catch prey in flight, but they spend most of their time waiting on leaves and plants. When they see prey, they zip out and grab it.

make them amazing—
and fast—flyers. They can
fly backward or forward. They can even
hover in place like a helicopter.

Fierce flying skills keep these insects
alive. They eat other flying insects, and
they catch their prey (the animals they

Halloween
pennant

eat) in midflight. So if a dragonfly can't fly, it will starve to death.

Great vision also helps dragonflies find their prey. Their large, compound eyes help them see in almost every direction—in front, behind, above, and below them. They can spot prey with their excellent vision and snatch it out of the air with their legs.

Dragonflies usually live near some form of water, such as a pond, stream, or river. A male dragonfly takes over a small area. This is called his territory. Males will fight one another to protect their territories.

Dragonflies are some of the largest flying insects. But some species of dragonflies are larger than others. The **giant darner** is the largest dragonfly in North America. Its body can be more than 4-1/2 inches long and it has a 5-inch wingspan. It lives near ponds and streams in the southwestern United States. The **common green darner** is smaller. It has a 3-inch-long body and a 4-1/2-inch wingspan. The **scarlet dwarf** is the smallest dragonfly. It has a 1/2-inch-long body and a 3/4-inch wingspan.

Giant darner

Common green darner

Scarlet dwarf

Like dragonflies, mayflies are also primitive-winged insects. They have very short lives. Adult mayflies may live for just a few minutes or for as long as a day. During that time, they find mates and females lay eggs. A mayfly's adult life is so short that it doesn't even have mouthparts. It won't live long enough to need a meal.

Mayflies lay their eggs in or on water. After they hatch, naiads can sometimes live underwater for three or four years.

They breathe with gills and feed on underwater plants and animals.

When they are ready to leave the water, mayflies crack open their exoskeleton. They emerge and shake out their wings. Then they are ready to fly.

Mayflies usually come out of the water in late spring or early fall, sometimes in enormous numbers. Dark clouds of the insects swarm into the sky. Some of these clouds are so huge that

they have been seen from weather satellites.

Mayflies don't travel far. Once their life cycle is over, they may pile up in huge drifts. After one swarm poured out of the

Mississippi River between Davenport, Iowa, and St. Paul, Minnesota, in 2014, snowplows were needed to clean up the dead mayflies.

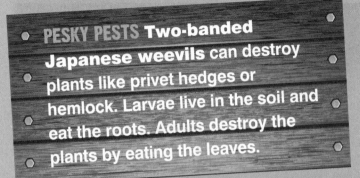

PESKY PESTS **Two-banded Japanese weevils** can destroy plants like privet hedges or hemlock. Larvae live in the soil and eat the roots. Adults destroy the plants by eating the leaves.

WHAT'S FOR DINNER?

Like all animals, insects must eat to live. What do they eat? Just about anything. Their meals may include meat, plants, garbage, seeds, and even dung.

Grasshoppers live in fields and meadows, and they eat plants. Termites live in logs, trees, and wooden houses, where they eat wood. Mantises living in the rain forest eat other insects and even small lizards and birds. Cockroaches have

Strawlike mouthparts

Grinding mouthparts

Spongy mouthparts

evolved to live well among humans. They will eat nearly anything, including the garbage we throw away.

That's *what* they eat. But how do they eat it?

Different insects have different ways to take in food. They don't have teeth, so they can't just chew up food and swallow it. But some insects have sharp mouthparts that act like teeth to grind up meat and plants. These sharp mouthparts are called mandibles (MAN-dih-bulls). They look like a pair of pliers, and are used to hold, cut, and bite food.

Insects with mandibles chomp their food over and over. When their food is small enough, they swallow it. Mandibles can grind up small animals or slice through leaves and flowers. The mandibles of a huge **titan beetle** are strong enough to cut a pencil in half.

Many insects have strawlike mouthparts called proboscises (pro-BOSS-is-es), which they use to eat liquid foods. A butterfly has a long, thin proboscis. It rolls this mouthpart out,

Titan beetle

reaches into a flower, and sips up the juicy nectar. This sucking motion is the main way many insects eat.

Other insects have both mandibles and a proboscis. Bees and wasps use mandibles to eat bits of plants or wood. They also use a proboscis to suck nectar from flowers.

When they want to eat, **assassin bugs** stab

A moth unrolls its long proboscis to eat.

other insects with a sharp proboscis. They spit their digestive fluids into the hole from the stab. This turns the prey into liquid. Then the assassin bug is able to suck up its meal.

Biting flies, such as house flies, don't really bite at all. Instead, they smush their prey with their flat, spongy mouthparts. Then they smear their saliva on the prey. As the prey dissolves, the fly swallows its liquid meal using its spongy mouth.

Some insects gather in huge groups to feed. This is called swarming. Insects such as ants, grasshoppers, and bees will sometimes swarm.

Locusts are the most well-known

FACT FILE: STAYING ALIVE

Insects have special tools for survival.

HIDING This **leaf butterfly** blends in using camouflage.

BUILT-IN PROTECTION Armor helps the **ironclad beetle** survive attacks by predators.

SELF-DEFENSE **Bombardier beetles** shoot out goo that burns their predators.

DISGUISE The **clearwing moth** looks like a wasp. Called mimicry, this trick fools predators.

swarming insects.
Millions of locusts can
swarm over farmland or grassland,
eating everything they find. In a short
time, they will eat all the plants in an
area. In Africa, locust swarms have
eaten half the food crops in some areas.
Scientists think some swarms can
include as many as 10 billion locusts.
That's a HUGE swarm!

Locusts

CAN YOU SPOT IT? The **Malaysian orchid mantis** hides among the orchid flowers of its rain forest home. When a butterfly or fly comes by, the mantis uses its lightning-quick front legs to snatch its prey.

MANTIDS, PHASMIDS, AND MORE

Praying mantises and walking sticks are unusually shaped insects that belong to different groups. Both of these groups are distantly related to insects such as grasshoppers, crickets, cockroaches, and termites.

Most mantids have long, thin bodies. They have triangle-shaped heads. Four of their legs are used for walking. Their front two legs act more like arms.

Mantids are ambush predators, which

means they lie in wait for prey. They can move their heads in almost a complete circle to see all around them. When prey is near, they use their strong front legs to grab it. Sharp spines on these legs help them grip and hold on. Then, they use their powerful mouthparts to crunch and bite.

With clever attack skills and sharp jaws, mantids can catch and eat many types of

The praying mantis gets its name from the way its front legs are held, making it look as if it is saying a prayer.

prey. They eat insects, as well as small lizards and frogs. Some mantid species will even eat other mantids.

Many species of mantids live in forests. Tropical forests are a particular favorite. But they can live anywhere that has trees and is warm most of the year.

Mantids often use camouflage to hide from prey. The beautiful Malaysian orchid mantis mimics, or looks just like, a pink

Dead leaf mantis

Ghost mantis

Moss mantis

flower. The moss mantis looks like what it's named for. It also can grow bumps to look like the wood where moss grows. The dead leaf mantis has the colors and veins of nearby leaves. The ghost mantis also mimics leaf patterns with its body. The **conehead mantis** looks like a stick and can hide on tree trunks and branches.

Stick insects are phasmids. They were once thought to be closely related to mantids. Like mantids, they have long, skinny bodies. They got their name from their appearance—they look like sticks. This makes them hard to spot in trees.

These masters of disguise come in a wide variety of sizes. Some stick insects are less than 1 inch long. The **giant walking stick** grows to nearly 2 feet long. When threatened, stick insects may play dead, hoping a predator will lose interest. If a predator grabs them by the leg, they may just leave the leg behind and run away on the rest of their legs.

Termites are famous for eating wood. They can't digest it themselves, but bacteria and other organisms that live in their stomachs can. In the wild, termites are very helpful. They break down rotten wood as they digest it, and their poop makes good soil for plants. Termites also dig nests in soil, and that helps water soak into the ground.

Stick insect

Some termites in Africa and Australia build nests above ground. These towers made from earth and termite spit can be more than 20 feet tall. The upper parts of the nest help circulate air, keeping the termites comfortable at the base where they live.

Millions of termites can live in a nest. The group is called a colony, and each member of the group has a job to do. The queen lays eggs. Worker termites build the nest. Soldiers guard against invaders.

When termites live among people, they eat the wood used to build houses and buildings. They can do great damage to the structure of a building.

Cockroaches have been around for 350 million years and are good at surviving.

While many say "Eww!" about cockroaches, we should also say "Thanks." Here are some of the ways that cockroaches are helpful to the world.

SCAVENGERS In the wild, cockroaches eat dead or decaying animals. They are  recyclers, and pass nutrients from the animals they eat into the soil and plants when they poop. Nitrogen is the most important nutrient cockroaches spread.

FOOD FOR OTHERS Insects, birds, reptiles, amphibians, and mammals eat cockroaches.

FOOD FOR PEOPLE In Asia, cockroaches are among the many insects sold as food. Often fried, they are inexpensive and high in protein.

RESEARCH AND LEARNING Entomologists (EN-tuh-MAH-luh-jists) are scientists who study insects. They observe live insects in the wild, study them in labs, and learn a lot by dissecting, or taking apart, dead cockroaches.

HOVERING HAWK The **hummingbird hawk moth** is often mistaken for a hummingbird because of the way it hovers in midair. It uses its long proboscis to suck up nectar from flowers.

MOVING AROUND

Whether they fly, run, walk, hop, or swim, insects have amazing abilities to get around. Each insect moves in the best way for it to find the food it needs to survive.

Nearly all insects have wings at some time in their lives. Some insects barely use their wings. Other insects rely on their wings as the main way they get around.

Many insects are awesome flyers. The hawk moth flaps its wings very fast, like a hummingbird, and hovers in front of a

Desert locust

plant to eat. Dragonflies are the ace pilots of the insect world. Their four wings let them fly in any direction. They have been clocked going as fast as 35 miles per hour.

Some types of grasshoppers can zoom along at more than 30 miles per hour. They use their powerful back legs to help them take off and fly. They also use strong muscles in their legs to hop. They can go about 3 feet in a single jump. That's pretty far

for an insect that's just 2 to 3 inches long!

Not all insects fly well. For example, crickets just hop. They have wings, but they don't use them. A **spider cricket** can cover a distance 60 times its body length in one leap. Other crickets average leaps about 30 times their body length. Fleas and bedbugs can't fly because they don't have wings. Instead, they hop or crawl from place to place.

Most insects can also walk or run. And mostly, they use all six legs for walking. But some also use their legs for other tasks. Mantids grab prey with their front two legs. **Camel crickets** have flat pads

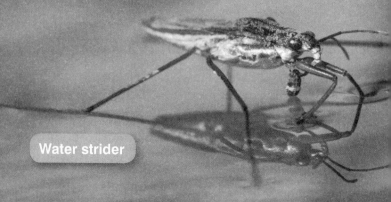

Water strider

on their front legs that they use to dig into the soil. Dragonflies can form their legs into a basket shape to hold prey. Some insects spend their time in or on water. Water striders are light enough that they can walk on the water's surface. They have special bristles on their four back legs. These bristles repel (push away) water. The bristles form a superthin layer on top of the water. The insects walk on that layer. Other insects, such as **water boatmen**, have legs with parts that work like paddles to move through the water. Some dragonfly naiads have a special way of getting around. They shoot water backward from their bodies. This makes them shoot forward.

Only a few adult insects can live in the water. **Diving beetles** have large pads on their front legs. They use these pads like paddles. They can duck under the surface of a pond and swim after prey.

FACT FILE: WALK THIS WAY

To walk, insects move three legs at a time. While they're lifting those three, they keep the other three legs on the ground. But if they moved all the legs on one side at the same time, they might tip over. So how do they walk?

Scientists used slow-motion cameras to study how insects walk.

For the first step, two legs on one side and one leg on the other side are on the

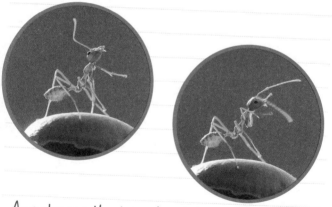

An ant uses the tripod gait to step gracefully from one mushroom cap to another.

ground. For the next step, insects use the legs they didn't use on the first step.

At slow speeds, the insect might lift one leg at a time while making this step pattern. Moving fast, it moves several legs at a time.

This pattern of how insect feet move is called a tripod gait. *Tripod* means "three legs," and *gait* means a way of walking.

Insects seem to have the same tripod gait no matter how fast or slow they are moving.

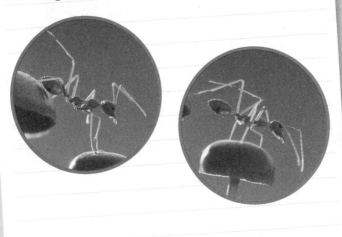

LIGHT THE WAY Fireflies make their abdomens light up by activating a chemical in their bodies. They light up the night sky to signal others and to attract mates.

MEET THE BEETLES

If the world's beetles had a meeting and everyone attended, they'd need a BIG room. There are more than 350,000 known species of beetles. Some experts think there might be more than half a million more beetle species that we haven't discovered yet.

Why are there so many types of beetles? Scientists point to the body armor of these insects. The hard shell really protects them. It lets the animals live in just about any habitat. They can crawl on and under the earth. They can live in trees. Some can even swim. Beetles now live on every continent except Antarctica.

Most beetles are round or oval. They have mouthparts that chomp food. They all have antennae with 11 or fewer segments. Beetles use their antennae to smell and sense movement in the air. They also use them like feelers, to find food and safe places to lay eggs.

As adults, all beetles have two pairs of wings. The outer

pair folds and meets in the center of the beetle's back. This forms the hard shell that protects the insect's flying wings and body. Beetles open up these outer wings when lifting off and taking flight. The delicate inner wings spread out for flight.

To reach adulthood, beetles go through complete metamorphosis. The babies, called larvae, often look like tiny worms.

The outer wings, called elytra (eh-LIE-truh), stay open and flap when beetles fly.

Some beetle larvae are called grubs. Most beetle larvae molt their outer skin as they grow. Eventually, the larvae form pupae, which are small, hard sacs that surround their bodies. Inside the pupa, the insect grows until it emerges as an adult beetle.

Beetles have amazing body parts. Tiger beetles walk high above the ground on long legs. They can run so fast on their long legs that they go temporarily blind—their vision can't keep up with their speed! How fast do they go? More than 1 mile per hour. That may not sound fast, but for a little beetle, it's super speedy.

Male **harlequin** (HAR-lih-kwin) **beetles** have front legs that are often longer than their bodies, which are about 3 inches

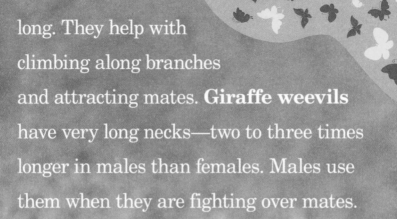

long. They help with climbing along branches and attracting mates. **Giraffe weevils** have very long necks—two to three times longer in males than females. Males use them when they are fighting over mates.

Big sand tiger beetles use their speed and mandibles to grab ants, flies, and other prey.

BIG BEETLES

TITAN BEETLES have
the largest bodies,
growing to more than
6 inches long. They
look fierce, and hiss
when threatened.

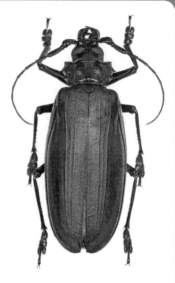

ACTAEON BEETLES
are about 5 inches
long. They have large
claws that they use to
grip and climb trees.

STAG BEETLES grow
to about 3 inches
long. Their giant
mandibles look
like deer antlers.

Giraffe weevils are named for their long necks.

The **doodlebug**'s antennae look like big orange fans.

Other amazing body parts give beetles impressive abilities, too. **Namib Desert beetles** have special organs on their skin that can collect tiny drops of water vapor from the air. Fireflies, also called lightning bugs, can light up their abdomens. When oxygen combines with a special substance in their bodies, they produce a light that flashes on and off.

Beetles come in a wide range of sizes. **Hercules beetles** are large at nearly 6 inches long. But other beetles are nearly microscopic. A featherwing beetle found in Colombia is just 1/100 of an inch long. That's smaller than a grain of salt.

Beetles come in many different colors, too. Some, like the **golden scarab beetle**, look like shining pieces of jewelry. The shells of jewel beetles shimmer with

Golden scarab

metallic colors. They are green, silver, or golden.

Some of the most well-known beetles, ladybugs, come in red, yellow, orange, and even gray. Whatever their color, ladybugs are easily recognized by the spots on their

Yellow ladybug

backs. They can have as many as twenty spots, or as few as two spots. (There's just one ladybug with no spots at all.)

There is even a beetle that has no color. The **cyphochilus beetle** is bright white. Its very thin shell reflects light completely. This is why it appears white.

EXTREME INSECTS

With about 1 million species, there are lots of insects to consider when looking for the biggest, loudest, or oldest. Here are a few. But this list could change. Scientists are finding new insects every day.

Goliath beetle

SOME OF THE WORLD'S LONGEST INSECTS

Chan's megastick insect 22 inches long

Titan beetle 6.5 inches long

Rhinoceros beetle 6 inches long

Actaeon beetle 5 inches long

African cicada

Queen
Alexandra's
birdwing

LOUDEST
African cicada 106.7 decibels (That's louder than a motorcycle!)

LARGEST WINGSPAN
Queen Alexandra's birdwing 11 to 12 inches

Atlas moth 11 to 12 inches

Giant helicopter dragonfly 7.5 inches

SOME OF THE WORLD'S HEAVIEST INSECTS
Goliath beetle 3.5 ounces

Giant weta 2.5 ounces

SMALLEST
Parasitoid wasp 6/1000 inch (That's smaller than a poppy seed.)

Chan's megastick insect

THE EYES HAVE IT Compound eyes make the **robber fly** one of the most ferocious predators of the insect world. Each eye has hundreds of individual lenses that help it see the world, and prey, clearly.

INSECT SENSES

Like other animals, insects have body parts that gather information. They have ways to hear, see, taste, touch, and smell. Insects need to find food and avoid danger. They need to look for mates. They have to move around and then find their way home. Insect senses are similar to other animals' senses, but the body parts they use are quite different.

The expression "bug-eyed" means having large, round eyes. The term comes from the insect world. Many insects have

DO INSECTS SEE COLOR?

IN LIVING COLOR

About a hundred years ago, a scientist named Karl Von Frisch discovered that bees can see some colors. He created a grid that included different colored squares. The bees could learn to find food if it was placed on a blue square. Since then, scientists have learned that insects' compound eyes can detect some color differences.

enormous compound eyes that cover large parts of their heads. Dragonflies have as many as 28,000 eye parts, called ommatidia, in each compound eye! These help them detect light, images, and motion. Compound eyes can't change their focus from near to far, the way human eyes can. But they can see many images at once.

Many species can sense a

type of light that is invisible to humans: ultraviolet light. This gives insects more information about their world. Ultraviolet light is part of sunlight, but human eyes cannot see it. (People can experience it, though—it causes suntans and burns.)

Some insects have simple eyes, or ocelli (oh-SELL-ee). Simple eyes look like small black bumps. They are usually on or near the top of the insect's head. Ocelli can sense light and dark. Bees and dragonflies are some of the insect species that have ocelli.

Some larvae have another kind of simple eye, called lateral ocelli. These are found on the side of the head. (Lateral means it's on the side of something.)

Ocelli

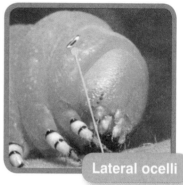
Lateral ocelli

Before a caterpillar turns into a butterfly, it has lateral ocelli. These eyes help the caterpillar see. When the caterpillar becomes an adult butterfly or moth, it will have compound eyes.

Nearly all insects have antennae. These important sense organs come in pairs. The antennae move and wave and gather sense information such as smell, taste, and touch. How do they work? They use chemoreception (KEE-moh-ree-SEPP-shun), which helps them "smell" chemicals in the air. (Sharks also use chemoreception to smell in the water.) Antennae can feel physical objects too, and detect movement nearby. Insects can use the information their antennae gather to find food. Fruit flies, for instance, use their antennae to detect the carbon dioxide given off by rotting fruit. That helps them find fruit that they can lay their eggs on.

Antennae come in almost as many shapes and sizes as the insects that have them. Some are tiny, while others are long. **Cave crickets** have antennae that are longer than their bodies. Some are smooth, and some are fuzzy. The antennae of some moths look like brushes.

Some insects also have bristles on their exoskeletons. They are not hairs, since insects don't have hair. But they are kind of like whiskers, and they react when touched. This gives the insect more information about the world around it.

Most insects sense sounds in the same way humans and many other animals do: They detect vibrations in the air created by sounds. Insects don't have ears, so they hear with other parts of their bodies. Katydids and grasshoppers have patches on their legs that vibrate (move back and forth very fast) in reaction to noise. These patches are called tympana (tim-PAH-nuh). Another way insects hear is through patches of skin on their antennae, called Johnston's organs. The patches vibrate when sound hits them. Fruit flies use these organs to detect the sounds of potential mates.

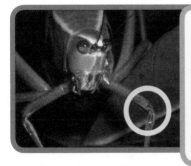

Katydids hear through tympana found on their legs. In humans, the tympanum—also called the eardrum—is located in the middle ear.

FACT FILE: LIKE A MOTH TO A FLAME

Many insects have senses that help them get around at night. You've probably seen moths fluttering around a porch light at night. Or you might spot them flying around near streetlights. Scientists have more than one theory about why moths are attracted to light.

Some scientists think that many moths find their way at night by observing the moon and the stars. There have been moths on Earth for millions of years, but lightbulbs have been around for only about a hundred years. Moths have not learned the difference between the light from a lightbulb and moonlight.

Moths sleep during the day. Some scientists think that they need to see the sun to know it's time to sleep. When they see a porch light, they believe it is daytime and head there to find a place to rest.

A third idea involves mating. One scientist found that lightbulb light is close to the slight glow produced by some female moths. But other scientists think the connection is not close enough to explain the behavior.

Why do you think moths fly to light?

I WANT TO SUCK YOUR BLOOD

Mosquitoes and flies stab their victims. Then they suck out liquid with a strawlike proboscis. Some have mouthparts like a sponge and sop up their food.

MOSQUITOES, FLIES, AND FLEAS

Though they are tiny, mosquitoes are the deadliest animals in the world. They carry germs that infect millions of people every year with diseases. Many people die from these diseases.

Adult female mosquitoes need blood to make their eggs. They use a sharp, pointed mouthpart to stab into prey. Then they suck out blood. When they stab, they transfer some blood from other animals. That blood can sometimes carry dangerous diseases.

Mosquito larvae underwater

Mosquitoes lay their eggs near water.
Ponds, streams, puddles, and rivers
are common mosquito breeding areas.
The more water, the more mosquitoes
breed. That's why wet, tropical areas
have so many mosquitoes. Central
Africa, Southeast Asia, and the
Caribbean are very active areas
for mosquitoes. Where there are
more mosquitoes, there is

more disease. Malaria, yellow fever, West Nile virus, and the Zika virus are some of the serious diseases spread by mosquitoes.

Flies are not as deadly to people as mosquitoes are. But they also carry diseases, including cholera. There are more than 150,000 species of flies in the world. Sometimes it seems like all of them are at your picnic, right? In their short adult life, flies can lay more than 1,000 eggs. And they live all around the world. Flies are common pests on farms, where they lay eggs in animal dung. When they bite the animals, they can also transmit diseases. Fortunately, bats, owls, and other animals eat insects such as flies. These predators are often welcome visitors to horse stables and barnyards.

Some flies are named for the type of animals they normally bite. These include **deer flies** and **horse flies**.

Not all flies look like **houseflies**. The **stalk-eyed fly** gets its name from the body parts on which its eyes are located. The **bluebottle fly** has a shimmering blue body. The **sand fly** has legs almost as long as its body.

Flies do some good: They

eat dead animals that would otherwise slowly rot away. Also, because fruit flies breed so quickly, scientists use them in experiments. Some of the most important discoveries in genetics

Stalk-eyed fly

(the science of how traits are passed from parents to offspring) have been made using fruit flies.

There is one kind of insect that really bugs our pets. Fleas live on other animals. They bite into the skin and suck out blood. The cat flea lives on the skin of cats and dogs. A species called a dog flea also lives on cats and dogs, but is far less common. When the fleas bite, it causes itching. When your pet starts scratching an area again and again, it's time to check for fleas. Fleas bite humans, too—especially around the feet and ankles.

Fleas can't fly, but they can jump— up to 7 inches high and 13 inches forward. When they land on an animal, they use their claws to hang on to the skin and hair. Hooks and barbs on their legs keep them from falling off when the animal moves. The bodies of fleas are flat. This helps them slip between strands of hair.

Dog flea

EPIC MIGRATION Monarchs travel south more than 3,000 miles to get to warm nesting areas. They fly during the day and rest at night. Thousands may cluster together on a single tree.

BUTTERFLIES AND MOTHS

There are 17,500 species of butterflies and 160,000 species of moths. Butterflies are perhaps more familiar, because they are most active during the day. Moths are most active at night.

All butterflies share certain features. Their bodies are long and slender. Four colorful wings and six legs are attached to their thoraxes. Atop their heads are skinny antennae. At the end of each antenna is a bulb called a club. Some butterflies dip

In some butterfly species, the two sides of the wings are different colors. When its wings are open, the **peacock butterfly** shows off bright colors and spots. When closed, a brown pattern helps it blend in.

these antennae ends into the soil to sniff out chemicals that might lead them to food.

Butterflies' wings have distinct color patterns, which are formed by tiny, overlapping scales. These colors help butterflies recognize mates from their own species. Some color patterns also act as camouflage from predators.

The Queen Alexandra's birdwing is the largest butterfly in the world. Its wings can be up to 12 inches across.

The smallest butterfly, the **western pygmy blue**, has wings that are only about 1/2 inch across.

Butterflies also have different wing shapes. Swallowtails have finger-shaped points sticking out from the bottom edges of their wings. **Zebra longwings** have upper wings that are much bigger than the lower wings.

Some butterflies do not live very long as adults. They don't even bother eating. They look for a mate and then die. Butterflies that do eat have a long, thin proboscis that curls into a spiral underneath their heads. When they visit flowers, the proboscis uncurls into a long straw for sipping nectar from the plant.

Clubbed antennae

Fanned antennae

Some species, including the **American painted lady**, eat rotting fruit. Others, such as the **purple emperor**, feast on decaying animal flesh.

Caterpillars (larvae) eat various kinds of plants. They increase in size thousands of times, which means they have to munch through a lot of leaves and other plant parts. They don't have wings, but they have legs and travel by walking. When they have eaten enough to survive the next stage of their

Pointed antennae

metamorphosis, they make their chrysalis. During this process, some caterpillars spin out a strong silk thread. This thread attaches to a leaf or branch to hold the chrysalis safely in place.

Moths are insects that are closely related to butterflies. They share many of the same body parts, but there are differences.

Moths are usually less brightly colored. Their bodies are often more plump than butterflies'. Their antennae end in fans or points. The **polyphemus** (pah-lee-FEE-mus) **silk moth** has wide, fan-shaped antennae. The fans are

Caterpillars have worm-like bodies that might have bristles, bumps, horns, or spikes. The **dagger moth caterpillar** has several pointy spikes that can sicken an animal that gets stuck by one. **Passion**

Dagger moth caterpillar

Passion butterfly caterpillar

butterfly caterpillar skin is studded with spikes. They are not poisonous, but the whole caterpillar is. Predators learn to avoid it.

Often the colors of the caterpillar are not the same as the colors of the adult butterfly. Some colors and patterns are camouflage to help protect the caterpillar. The **brimstone butterfly caterpillar** is green to match the leaves it lives on. The **wavy-lined emerald caterpillar** covers its body with the flowers it is eating, so it hides among its food.

Brimstone caterpillar

broad, and look almost like leaves. Their size increases the moth's ability to pick up scents. Australia's **white antennae tiger moth** has antennae that end in points.

Like butterflies, moth larvae are caterpillars. They spin a soft sac called a cocoon. Inside, they go through metamorphosis. The adult moth then emerges.

Moths are not nearly as pesky as flies or mosquitoes. They can cause trouble, however. **Gypsy moth** larvae infest and kill trees. **Clothes moths**—caterpillars and adults—eat fabrics such as wool. Some caterpillars, such as those of the **puss moth**, have spines or can shoot out stinging goo if attacked.

SPEED TRAP Trap-jaw ants have the world's fastest mouths. They can snap their jaws together at up to 145 miles per hour. They can also use that snapping power to launch themselves into the air to escape a predator.

ANTS, BEES, AND WASPS

Ants, bees, and wasps have many things in common. They share physical traits and behave in similar ways. They have three body parts that are easy to spot. This is especially true in ants. All ants go through complete metamorphosis. Only queens and drones have wings. Queens have them for a short time, and drones for their entire lives. The vast majority of ants in a colony are workers that never have wings at any point in their life.

Ants, bees, and wasps are social insects. Most live in large colonies or nests. In a colony, the queen rules. She lays nearly all the eggs. All the other insects in the colony are there to keep her alive.

Nests can include millions of individual ants. Ants build them underground, in mounds, in trees or logs, or even in buildings. Like other social insects, ants work really well as a team. In large groups or small, they combine their strength and skills.

Leaf-cutter ants work together to cut leaves used to line their home. An individual

leaf-cutter ant can pick up a piece of a plant that weighs much more than it does. The ants carry the leaves back to the colony. In the nest, the leaves grow fungus for the ants to eat.

Some ants do important jobs. As scavengers, they eat rotting dead animals and plants. Their underground nests help get air into the soil, making it richer. They are a food source for many animals, including lizards, frogs, snakes, and—of course—anteaters.

Some ants can cause real trouble,

Leaf-cutter ants

Army ants

though. **Army ants** will attack anything they come across, including small animals. **Fire ants** attack in great numbers, too. They can be fatal to people who are allergic to their stings. **Bulldog ants** in Australia do not have a bad bite, despite their large jaws, but they do have very potent stings that can cause human deaths.

Bees build their hives to protect the queen bee. Worker bees leave the hive to visit flowers. They eat the nectar and collect plant pollen that sticks to their bodies.

As the bees move from flower to flower, they spread the pollen. This helps plants reproduce, including trees, flowers, and many fruit and vegetable crops. This process, called pollination, is important for plants, including many that we eat. Bees produce honey in their hives. The hives themselves are made of a wax that can be used to make candles and other products.

Bees are excellent parents. The queen lays her eggs inside the hive. Then adult bees tend the eggs until they hatch. The larvae are fed honey made by the adults.

This honeybee is "wearing" lots of yellow pollen.

Paper wasp nest

Mud dauber nest

Yellowjacket nest

Many wasps are builders that create interesting nests. Some use mud to attach the nest to leaves, logs, or structures. Paper wasps build nests with many chambers inside. These chambers are used as places for laying eggs. Some yellowjackets build nests underground, like ants.

Most wasps don't stay with their young, but they have ways of making sure their babies will have food to eat. Sometimes they will bring other insects to their nest as food for their young. Caterpillars are common, if unwilling, food for wasp larvae.

A female **tarantula hawk wasp** hunts tarantulas. When she finds one, she stings it and drags the paralyzed spider—much larger than she is—to an underground burrow. Then she lays one egg on it, covers up the burrow, and leaves. When the egg hatches, the larva feeds on the tarantula. The female chooses one spider for each egg she lays.

Tarantula hawk wasp

AN ARMY OF ANTS

In every ant colony, there are different types of ants that do different jobs.

QUEEN This female is the largest ant in the colony. She lays all the eggs. Some queen ants can lay thousands of eggs at a time. If a new queen is born, she will soon leave the nest to start her own colony. These are called princess ants.

WORKERS Worker ants are all females that can't lay eggs. They gather food for the colony. They never have wings.

DRONES These male ants exist to fertilize the queen. They have wings, so they can travel farther away from the nest to mate with other queen ants.

SOLDIERS These female ants work to protect the colony. Sometimes they raid other colonies, like pirates of the ant world.

These **safari ant** soldiers guard the worker ants in the colony.

RESOURCES

There are many good ways to get close to insects and learn more, including visiting them at a museum, reading books like this one, and joining organizations dedicated to studying insects.

MUSEUMS WITH INSECTS

Natural History Museum of Los Angeles County
Los Angeles, California
nhm.org

California Academy of Sciences
San Francisco, California
calacademy.org

The Field Museum
Chicago, Illinois
fieldmuseum.org

University of Kansas Natural History Museum
Lawrence, Kansas
naturalhistory.ku.edu

Harvard Museum of Natural History
Cambridge, Massachusetts
hmnh.harvard.edu

Insectropolis
Toms River, New Jersey
insectropolis.com

American Museum of Natural History
New York, New York
amnh.org

Smithsonian National Museum of Natural History
Washington, D.C.
mnh.si.edu

NONFICTION BOOKS

Bugopedia: The Complete Guide to Everything Insect Plus Other Creepy Crawlies, by the Discovery Channel (Discovery/Time)

Eyewitness Insects, by Laurence Mound (DK Publishing)

Kaufman Field Guide to Insects of North America, by Eric R. Eaton and Kenn Kaufman (Houghton Mifflin)

Smithsonian Handbook: Insects, by George C. McGavin (Smithsonian Press)

FICTION FAVORITES

Charlotte's Web, by E.B. White (Harper & Brothers)

James and the Giant Peach, by Roald Dahl (Alfred A. Knopf, Inc)

ORGANIZATIONS

Entomological Society of America
entsoc.org

North American Butterfly Association
naba.org

Amateur Entomologists' Society kids page
amentsoc.org/bug-club

Dragonhead caterpillar

MEET THE INSECT ORDERS

Scientists have divided all the insects in the world into 31 groups called orders. Within each order, the insects are divided into families. Within each family, there are genera (genus), which have even more similar features. Within each genus, there are species; there is only one type of insect in each species. This book introduces species in 13 insect orders. They are listed below. Since the numbers of species of insects described by science increases every day, the exact number of species in each order is continuously changing. The numbers below are estimates.

ODONATA 5,680 species in this order, including common green darner, giant darner, giant helicopter dragonfly, Halloween pennant dragonfly, Kirby's dropwing dragonfly, and scarlet dwarf

ISOPTERA 2,864 species in this order, including termites; some scientists put termites in the same order as cockroaches

BLATTODEA 4,565 species in this order, including the cockroach family

MANTODEA 2,384 species in this order, including conehead mantis, dead leaf mantis, ghost mantis, Malaysian orchid mantis, praying mantis, and moss mantis

PHASMATODEA 2,853 species in this order, including Chan's megastick insect, and giant walking stick

ORTHOPTERA 23,616 species in this order, including camel cricket, cave cricket, desert locust, elegant grasshopper, long-headed grasshopper, and spider cricket

HEMIPTERA 100,428 species in this order, including African cicada, green cicada, milkweed bug, stink bug, water boatman, and water strider

COLEOPTERA 359,891 species in this order, including actaeon beetle, big sand tiger beetle, bombardier beetle, cyphochilus beetle, diving beetle, doodlebug, dung beetle, firefly, giraffe weevil, golden scarab beetle, Goliath beetle, harlequin beetle, Hercules beetle, ironclad beetle, Japanese two-banded weevil, ladybug, maybug, Namib Desert beetle, rhinoceros beetle, stag beetle, titan beetle, and yellow ladybug

DIPTERA 152,244 species in this order, including blowfly, bluebottle fly, deer fly, fruit fly, horsefly, housefly, robber fly, sand fly, and stalk-eyed fly

SIPHONAPTERA 2,048 species in this order, including cat flea and dog flea

TRICHOPTERA 12,868 species in this order, including caddis fly

LEPIDOPTERA 156,793 species in this order, including American painted lady, arctic woolly bear caterpillar, Atlas moth, bee hawk moth, blue morpho butterfly, brimstone butterfly caterpillar, cecropia moth, clearwing moth, clothes moth, dagger moth caterpillar, gypsy moth, leaf butterfly, monarch butterfly, passion butterfly caterpillar, peacock butterfly, polyphemus silk moth, purple emperor, puss moth, Queen Alexandra's birdwing, wavy-lined emerald caterpillar, western pygmy blue, white antennae tiger moth, and zebra longwing

HYMENOPTERA 144,695 species in this order, including army ant, bull ant, fire ant, honeybee, leaf-cutter ant, mud dauber, paper wasp, parasitoid wasp, safari ant, tarantula hawk wasp, trap-jaw ant, and yellowjacket

INDEX

Illustrations are indicated by **boldface**. When they fall within a page span, the entire span is **boldface**.

CREDITS AND ACKNOWLEDGMENTS

Writer James Buckley, Jr.
Produced by Scout Books & Media Inc
President and Project Director Susan Knopf
Project Manager Brittany Gialanella
Copyeditor Beth Adelman
Proofreader Chelsea Burris
Designer Annemarie Redmond
Advisor Kenneth P. Wray

Thanks to the Time Inc. Books team: Margot Schupf, Anja Schmidt, Beth Sutinis, Deirdre Langeland, Georgia Morrissey, Megan Pearlman, Nina Reed, and Hillary Leary.

Special thanks to the Discovery and Animal Planet Creative and Licensing teams: Denny Chen, Carolann Dunn, Elizabeta Ealy, Summer Herrmann, Christina Lynch, Robert Marick, Doris Miller, and Janet Tsuei.